Little Children's Bible Books

JESUS' MIRACLES

Retold by Anne de Graaf   Illustrated by José Pérez Montero

BROADMAN
&HOLMAN
PUBLISHERS

T3-BPD-785

JESUS' MIRACLES

Published in 2000 by Broadman & Holman Publishers,
Nashville, Tennessee

Text copyright © 2000 Anne de Graaf
Illustration copyright © 2000 José Pérez Montero
Design by Ben Alex
Conceived, designed and produced by
Scandinavia Publishing House

Printed in Hong Kong
ISBN 0-8054-2178-5

*Dedicated to Pedro Pérez Rollán
and to Channa Lauryn Potter*

Mary once asked Jesus to help at a wedding where there was no more wine. So Jesus turned water into wine!

A miracle is something God makes happen. Sometimes people think it's impossible, and sometimes not. When the sun came up this morning, that was a miracle from God.

7

Once, when Jesus was inside a house teaching, somebody cut a hole in the ceiling! Four men lowered a man down who could not walk. Jesus made him better.

Reach up high and try to touch your ceiling. Do you need some help?

9

There once was a man who had been sick for 38 years. Jesus asked him, "Do you want to get better? Then pick up your bed and walk." Jesus made the man well.

11

When Jesus saw a man with a shriveled hand, he said, "Stretch out your hand!" The man did so, and his hand became normal, just like the other one.

People came from all over, asking Jesus to heal them. There were so many sick and blind and disabled people that Jesus had to get into a boat to see them all.

Think of someone you know who is sick. You can ask Jesus to make him or her better. Jesus wants us to ask him for help.

15

There were two men who had always been blind. Jesus put his hands on their eyes and made them better.

Close your eyes and walk around the room. Jesus made these men better so they could see. Seeing is ANOTHER miracle of God.

One evening Jesus and his friends climbed into a fishing boat. "We will cross to the other side of the lake," Jesus promised them.

Jesus walked on water when his friends were caught in a storm at sea. He walked right out to meet them because they were afraid.

Try to walk on water in a rain puddle, but hold some-one's hand. Careful, don't slip!

27

Peter tried to walk on water like Jesus. He climbed over the side of the boat . . . and did not sink! But then the wind scared him, and when he began to sink, Jesus saved him.

Climb out of your bed or off a chair like Peter climbed out of the boat. Now make a sound like a HUGE wind.

Jesus covered a blind man's eyes with his hands. When Jesus took his hands away, the man said, "I see men, moving like trees." Then Jesus covered his eyes a second time, and the man could see!

Ask the person reading to
you to move like a tree.
Make your eyes small.
Now open them wide!

Jesus took Peter, James, and John up to a mountaintop. Then Moses and Elijah came down from heaven to talk with Jesus, just like old friends!

Can you name a friend who came to visit you lately?

There once were ten very sick men. "Please help us!" they begged Jesus. So Jesus did. He made them better. But only one of the ten came back to thank Jesus.

What happened to the others? Can you think of a miracle Jesus did for you that you can thank him for?

35

Mary, Martha, and their brother Lazarus were all good friends of Jesus. Once, when Jesus was gone, Lazarus became very sick and died. But Jesus came back and made Lazarus live again!

What is a miracle? YOU are a miracle! Jesus made you a special creation and that is the most special miracle of all!

A NOTE TO THE big PEOPLE:

The *Little Children's Bible Books* may be your child's first introduction to the Bible, God's Word. This story of *Jesus' Miracles* makes the four Gospels spring to life. This is a DO book. Point things out and ask your child to find, seek, say, and discover.

Before you read these stories, pray that your child's little heart would be touched by the love of God. These stories are about planting seeds, having vision, learning right from wrong, and choosing to believe. Pray together after you read this. There's no better way for big people to learn from little people.

A little something fun is said in italics by the narrating animal to make the story come alive. In this DO book, wave, wink, hop, roar, or do any of the other things the stories suggest so this can become a fun time of growing closer.